Homemade Pasta Dough

How to make pasta dough for the best pasta dough recipe including pasta dough for ravioli and other fresh pasta dough recipe ideas

Elisabetta Parisi

First Printing, 2012

ISBN-13: 978-1478234586

ISBN-10: 147823458X

Printed in the United States of America

Dedication

For Titus: hoping that he follows in my footsteps

Homemade Pasta Dough

How to make pasta dough for the best pasta dough recipe including pasta dough for ravioli and other fresh pasta dough recipe ideas

Table of Contents

Introduction

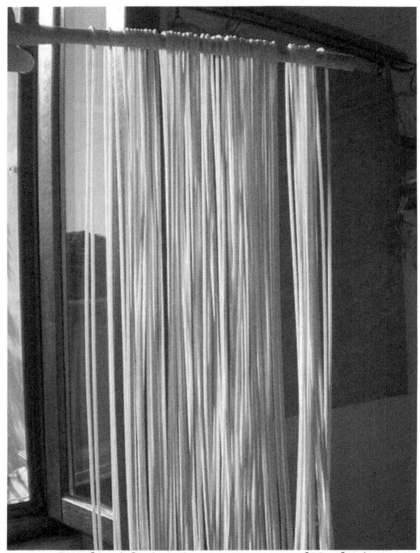

Spaghetti drying: image courtesy of Nnaluci

Most people end up buying pre-prepared pasta when they are making their favorite Italian dishes. This, of course, is very convenient and time saving. In the supermarket there are 2 forms of pre-prepared pasta that you can buy. There is the dried version, which is for sale everywhere, and then in larger supermarkets there are various versions of fresh pasta. These tend to be a little more expensive, but when you compare the two you will be amazed in the difference in both the taste and the texture of these two different pastas. The fresh pasta always comes out on top. That is the way it is, no competition. Therefore, you can see that fresh made pasta makes such a difference. We have become so complacent when it comes to pasta, that the first thing we reach for is the dried version.

Taking this a stage further, just think what the difference would be between the pasta that the supermarket mass produces and the pasta that you can create freshly in your own home. You can't get any fresher than the pasta you make yourself; it won't have preservatives or flavor enhancers; it will be just good honest pasta. In addition to this you can make the pasta the way you like it and use ingredients that are the best quality. In short, you can experiment with different flours and other ingredients until you come up with your own speciality pastas. Supermarkets can really only make pastas based on very basic dough ingredients. They couldn't possibly provide a full variety of pasta dough recipes because they would never be able to sell them all. They are, therefore, stuck with selling just the basic ones that they know they can sell before the expiry date.

Pasta dough making, and then the transformation into different shapes and designs that you can use in your cooking, is both satisfying for your mind and stomach. Making pasta dough doesn't have to be difficult either. You can make it completely by hand with simple equipment such as a mixing bowl, spoon and rolling pin. This can be a little time consuming and as a result you can speed up the process and make it easier by using some kitchen technology such as food processers and mixers. You can also buy specialized equipment such as pasta rollers and drying racks to get things done even more quickly and reliably. There is even a machine that will do everything for you. In this book I am going to describe basic pasta dough recipes for you to try, and then go on to show how you can produce more speciality pasta dough.

Using machines or making pasta by hand?

Pasta can be made entirely by hand, totally by machine or a mixture of both. Making the pasta by hand can be hard work and you will certainly work up a sweat doing the rolling part. Some people say that all of this effort adds to the satisfaction that you get when the product is finished and you get to taste the result.

Rolling the dough takes the most effort so having a rolling machine to do this can make your life easier. There are 2 kinds of pasta rolling machines. One is operated by hand where as the other is operated by an electric motor turning the rollers. There are lots of different models and they aren't that expensive. They can save time and a lot of effort on your part. These machines are limited to making flat style pastas and as a result extra work is required if you want different shapes.

There are also machines that can be used to take the hard work out of the mixing of the dough. Mixers to do this usually have a dough hook which helps to form the ball shape that you need. However, an ordinary food processor can be made to do just as good a job.

There are also pasta machines which virtually do the whole job. You just put the ingredients in the bowl of the machine, turn it on and it will do it all for you. These machines have various nozzles which will allow you to produce different shaped pasta such as the tubes in penne pasta

The basic pasta dough recipe

You can make pasta dough in its simplest form with just flour, oil and water. However, it is usual to add eggs to the mixture. The basic recipe here, therefore, uses eggs. There is an egg free recipe given later on in the book.

Ingredients

2 cups Semolina Flour or low gluten flour
2 eggs
½ tsp Salt
Water to moisten the dough

This is a very basic dough which is suitable for use with all kinds of different sauces.

The difference between using the 2 flour alternatives is that the one using the semolina flour is going to be more chewier when compared to the one using the low gluten flour.

Making the dough by hand

Making pasta by hand isn't difficult. Firstly make a mound of the flour on a flat surface which isn't porous. This could be the kitchen unit work surface or a plastic cutting board. Next you should make a well in the mound of flour. You could use a spoon, your hand, or a large ladle to do this. Once you have done this pour the eggs into the well. Slowly mix the eggs into the flour using a fork. You should gradually drag small amounts of flour from the edge of the well into the mixture.

Add salt to taste. Salt will help to bring out the flavor of the pasta, but don't put too much in as too much salt in the diet is unhealthy.

Knead the mixture using your hands adding more semolina flour as you work the dough. Sprinkle the work surface with semolina and put the mixed dough on the dusted surface. Sprinkle some more of the semolina flour over the dough and continue to knead it. Continue kneading the dough until it nice and smooth and quite firm. If the dough gets too dry and crumbly you can spray it with a little water and continue mixing until you get the right consistency. Don't be tempted to do too little kneading because the dough is likely to tear when you are rolling it out.

When you can place the dough on a clean part of the work surface and it doesn't stick it means that it is ready to be shaped. The smoothness of the dough will depend on the grind of the semolina. The finer the grind of the flour the smoother the dough will be.

Make the dough up into portions suitable for making sheets of pasta. It is easier to deal with smaller amounts of pasta dough, so it is best to try and make balls of dough that are about the size of a tennis ball. Once you are more experienced at forming the dough you can try using larger balls of the dough during the shaping process.

You need to allow the pasta dough to rest so that the gluten in the dough has a chance to relax. The best way to do this is to put the balls of dough in plastic wrap and leave them to sit at room temperature for about an hour. This process will make the pasta dough far easier to work, by stopping it from shrinking and springing back as it is stretched.

Rolling the dough by hand

This is the hard part. Firstly divide the dough into two pieces. Flour your work surface and start to roll out the dough using a rolling pin. Roll from the middle and flip it occasionally. Make sure that you flour it as needed to keep it from sticking to the surface. To stop the sheet from breaking when it has reached a large size you should roll it up around the rolling pin and then turn the rolling pin over. As you unroll the sheet of pasta gently stretch it by holding the unrolled part firmly and then pull softly away with the rolling pin. Carry on flipping and rolling the pasta until the sheet is almost transparent.

Using a mixer to make the dough

The use of an electric mixer makes the process of making pasta dough even easier. You use the same ingredients as given for the hand made dough above. Use the dough hook provided with your mixer.

Firstly add the flour to the machine's mixing bowl. Set the mixer to a slow speed and then begin to add the eggs. Add salt to taste as in the hand made method. Use the mixer to knead the dough until it is smooth, dry and very firm. If the dough gets too dry and crumbly you can spray it with a little water and continue mixing until you get the right consistency. However, don't allow the dough to become even a little wet as it will cause problems when you try to form it into sheets. The dough should stick to itself but to nothing else. If it is too wet it will stick to everything. If the dough is still sticky you should go on to knead it by hand and add extra semolina flour as in the hand made method until once again the dough is smooth and very firm.

When you can place the dough on a clean part of the work surface and it doesn't stick it means that it is ready to be shaped.

Make the dough up into portions suitable for making sheets of pasta. It is easier to deal with smaller amounts of pasta dough so it is best to try and make balls of dough that are about the size of a tennis ball.

Allow the pasta dough to rest so that the gluten in the dough has a chance to relax. Put the balls of dough in plastic wrap and leave them to sit at room temperature for about an hour.

Rolling the dough using a machine

Start by taking the pasta ball out of the plastic wrap. First, place dough on a flour dusted work surface and then press the ball of dough down with your hand. Use a rolling pin to roll out the dough until it is about 12 or 13 inches long. Cut the dough up into 3 pieces and pass one of them through the rollers at the machines widest setting. Reduce the width by 1 setting and pass the dough through again. Fold this dough up so that you have a rectangle shape. Reduce the setting of the machine by 1 again and pass the dough through the rollers. If the dough shows any sign of sticking, you should dust flour onto both sides of the pasta sheet before passing it through the machine again. Continue to reduce the width setting of the rollers and pass the dough through the machine until you have the thickness of pasta sheet that you want. Remember that pasta almost doubles in size during cooking.

Semolina based pasta as an aid to nutrition

Pasta is a benefit to any diet, especially when it is made from the correct ingredients. It contains valuable macro and micro nutrients. The main ingredient in pasta is semolina flour. This is coarse ground flour made from durum wheat. This is a high protein hard wheat which is amber colored. It is especially grown for making semolina pasta. Due to the high protein content it has a lower starch content compared to all purpose flour and is more easily digested.

Semolina based pasta has carbohydrates in the form of starch which means that it is more slowly digested compared to sugar rich carbohydrates. Pasta benefits from a low fat content and has no saturated fats. This is really good for people on diets. It also contains iron and the vitamins Thiamin, Niacin, Riboflavin and Folic acid. You should therefore relish having pasta in your diet because it is both very nutritional and good for you too.

Pasta Dough recipe using all purpose flour

For some types of pasta there is a need to use different dough recipes so that the dough can be formed more easily.

You can make pasta using standard all purpose flour. It will have different characteristics to the low gluten flour and semolina versions.

Ingredients

1¾ cups all purpose flour
1 tsp Salt
3 eggs
1 tsp Olive Oil

Method

You use the same method as given above for the basic dough adding the oil at the same time as the eggs.

You will find this dough recipe easier to deal with. The kneading process is a lot easier as the dough has a tenderer feel to it. However, this is also a bit of a disadvantage when it comes to kneading because, if you aren't careful, it can quickly become too sticky. Due to the extra gluten in all purpose flour you should allow the pasta to relax for a longer time. You should find that letting it sit in the plastic wrap for about an hour or more should be about right. When the pasta sheets have been made you have to be careful when cutting them, because it seems to tear a lot more easily. To get round this, you can try setting the pasta roller machine to a thicker setting than you would use with semolina pasta. It also cooks a lot faster too.

Pasta dough recipe without eggs

Pasta without eggs has the benefit of having mainly just the nutrition provided by the pasta flour. Eggs contain fat, especially in the yolk part, and as a result this pasta recipe can be seen as a low fat high protein food suitable for slimmer's on certain types of diet.

Ingredients

3 cups semolina flour
2 tbsp olive oil
1 cup warm water
½ tsp salt

Method

Place the semolina flour in large mixing bowl and then make a well in the center. Add the rest of the ingredients to the well and very slowly mix them together using a fork. Drag in the flour a little at a time in order to get a smooth and even mixture. Spend time on this and be patient so that you get a good result. After you have obtained a smooth mixture knead it by hand for about 10 minutes. If the mixture gets sticky add some extra flour. Let the dough rest for about 30 minutes and then repeat the kneading process a few times until you have smooth and silky dough. Place the dough ball in plastic wrap, until you are ready to use it. You can then go on to shape the pasta, either by hand or using a machine, as explained earlier.

Colored pasta

You don't have to stick to the usual pale yellow color of pasta. You can add various ingredients to the pasta dough, which will then produce a range of colors. Natural vegetables are ideal things to add, as this has been done for centuries. The addition of vegetables can change the characteristics of the dough making it lose its elastic nature and therefore more difficult to roll out into sheets. This can mean that the sheets have to be a bit thicker so that they won't break up. Vegetable material will also add water to the dough so you have to use a lot more judgment when it comes to the amount of flour to add. However, the usual rules apply if the dough is sticky then you simply add more flour until it becomes firm once again.

Green pasta

This is the typical alternative color for pasta that we see in shops and restaurants. You can use it with other colors such as red and yellow to make 'tricolore' pasta. It is also often served with cream sauces which can also be made to be green. Green pasta is also good as an alternative for making ravioli or lasagna. The green color is actually produced by adding spinach to the dough mixture. Spinach will also add valuable minerals to your pasta.

Ingredients

2 cups Flour

6 ounces raw spinach
2 eggs
Pinch of salt

Method

First of all, wash the spinach well and then drain it. Coarsely chop the spinach and then heat it in a saucepan with a very small amount of water. Add the salt and stir the spinach as it heats for about 4 minutes. When the spinach has cooled press it and squeeze it to remove a lot of the moisture. Put the spinach into a blender and puree it. Mix the puree in with the other ingredients when you make the dough.

Red pasta

Ingredients

2 cups Flour
2 tbsp tomato puree
2 eggs
Pinch of salt

Method

Heat the tomato puree gently in a saucepan to drive off as much water as you can without burning the tomato paste. Mix this with the other ingredients, used to make the dough, when you are stirring the eggs into the flour. Make sure that the red color is evenly distributed throughout the dough. For a deeper red color simply use more of the tomato puree. The more puree you use in this recipe the more acidic that the pasta will become. As a result this type of pasta is best used with sweeter creamier sauces to balance out the acidic nature of the tomato content. If you want a paler red that isn't as acidic you can try using some pureed cooked carrots and reduce the tomato paste down to only 1 tablespoon.

Dark red or purple pasta

Ingredients

2-3 cups Flour
1 large beetroot
2 eggs
Pinch of salt

Method

You can use fresh beetroot or cooked beetroot. In the case of fresh beetroot you need to boil it first and then remove the skin. After cooking dice the beetroot and blend it to a puree in a blender. Beetroot contains a lot of water so you need to use a fine muslin bag to squeeze as much water out of it as you can. Add the remaining beetroot paste to the pasta dough when you are mixing it up.

Other colors for pasta

There are a number of other colors that can be attempted. Black pasta can be achieved by adding squid ink. You can get a different yellow color by adding turmeric or even a dry cheese such as Parmigiano. Powdered baking chocolate can be used to produce brown pasta and orange pasta can be made by using cooked and pureed squash or pumpkin.

Herb, Spice and lemon pastas

Herb pasta

Ingredients
2cups Flour
Fresh herbs
2 eggs
Pinch of salt

Method

You need about 5 tablespoons of finely chopped fresh herbs. You can use just about any fresh herbs but certainly try sage, parsley, rosemary and thyme and anything else that takes your fancy. Combine the herbs with the eggs just before mixing the dough. There's no need to cook or puree fresh herbs. Herbs can be used on their own or in any combination. You should, however, think about which sauce you want to use with the herb pasta and consider whether they will work well together.

Roasted capsicum pepper pasta

You can use whichever color capsicum bell peppers that you like for this recipe. Red peppers are my choice but you could equally use green or yellow versions. The pasta will take on the color and flavor of the peppers. The pasta ends up with quite a subtle flavor and as a result is great with lighter sauces. The pasta will also take on the colors of the pasta too and as a result you can end up with flavored tricolor pasta if you use all three kinds of pepper.

Ingredients

1 cup of pureed roasted bell pepper
2 large eggs
1 tbsp extra virgin olive oil
1 tsp salt
2 ¾ cups plain flour

Once you have roasted the bell pepper then simply puree it in a food processor or blender.

Put the pureed bell pepper and the olive oil into a food processor or blender and whizz them up until you have a nice smooth mixture. Add the eggs to the mixture in the processor and whizz up again until they are just blended.

Add the flour and salt and then either mix in the food processor or do it by hand in a large bowl using a fork. Once you have a soft dough ball transfer it to a lightly floured work surface of board and knead until the dough is elastic and smooth. Add more flour if you can't reach the right consistency. Cover the kneaded dough with plastic wrap and leave it to stand for at least a half hour before proceeding to roll and cut it into the shapes that you want.

Lemon pasta

Ingredients
2 cups Semolina Flour
2 eggs and 1 egg yolk
Lemon juice
Lemon zest
½ tsp Salt

Method

Use the method given for the basic pasta dough but in addition to the 2 eggs adds an extra egg yolk. Add 2 tablespoons of lemon juice and 3 tablespoons finely grated lemon zest and then mix and knead the dough as usual.

Lemon and black pepper pasta

This pasta using plain flour is superb when served with sea food. Lemon is always a good choice to accompany sea food but in this case the black pepper gives a lot of extra bite and flavor.

Ingredients

2 ½ cups plain flour
2 whole large eggs
1 large egg yolk
1 tsp salt
1 teaspoon extra virgin olive oil
1 tsp water
3 tbsp finely grated lemon zest
1 tsp course freshly ground black pepper

Method

Put 2 cups of the plain flour, eggs, egg yolk, salt, olive oil, water, lemon zest and black pepper into a food processor and then blend them together well. Blend until the mixture starts to form a ball of dough.

Lightly flour a work surface and then knead the ball of dough. Add extra flour from the ½ cup left as you knead the dough. Continue until the dough becomes elastic and nice and smooth. Let the dough stand at room temperature for about 60 minutes. After this time you can roll it out and cut it to the shapes that you want.

Lemon and Parsley Pasta

Try this light flavored lemon parsley pasta. The best part of making your own pasta is being able to flavor it any way you like.

Ingredients

¼ cup chopped fresh parsley
2 tbsp lemon juice
1 tsp grated lemon zest
2 large eggs
1 tbsp extra virgin olive oil
1 tsp salt
2 cups plain flour

Method

Sift the flour into a large bowl and then make a well in the centre of it. Next put the eggs, chopped parsley, lemon juice, olive oil and lemon zest into the well. Use a fork to mix the well contents together and as you do so slowly drag in flour from the sides of the well.

Once a soft dough has formed transfer it to a lightly floured work surface or board and knead until a smooth and elastic dough is achieved. Cover the dough in plastic film and leave to stand for at least half an hour before continuing on to roll and cut it into the shapes that you require.

This pasta has a light flavor and is good to accompany fish dishes with light sauces.

Pasta with saffron

½ tsp. saffron thread, crushed to powder
½ tbsp. warm water
2 cups of all purpose flour
¼ tsp. salt
2 large eggs

This will make very yellow pasta with the distinctive taste of the saffron spice. The first thing to do is to crush the saffron threads to a powder using a pestle and mortar. You should then dissolve the crushed saffron in the warm water. Add the saffron water to the mixture, after adding the eggs to the well in the flour using the same method as for the basic pasta recipe above.

Noodle and whole wheat pastas

Egg noodle pasta

Ingredients

2 cups flour
½ teaspoon salt
2 teaspoons baking powder
3 eggs

Method

Use the basic method to mix the dough. Add water or flour if required in order to make dough that is stiff and workable. Place the dough on a board dusted with flour and then knead until smooth. Once complete, divide the dough into 3 pieces and roll each one until it is thin. Dust each sheet lightly with flour and then cut into strips. You should let the strips dry a little before cooking. To make the noodles more oriental and softer in nature increase the eggs to 4 but only use the yolks of each egg.

Pasta Noodles

Pasta dough made from whole wheat

Although pasta dough can be made using just whole wheat flour it tends to be very sticky and has a grainy texture. It is therefore best to mix it with all purpose flour which makes smoother dough due to its extra gluten content.

Ingredients

1 cup whole wheat flour
1 cup all-purpose flour
2 eggs
¼ teaspoon salt

1 tablespoon olive oil
2 tablespoons warm water

Method

Make the dough in the same way as the basic dough recipe given at the start of the book. If you need to add extra flour to prevent sticking then you should use the all purpose flour.

Whole wheat pasta has a different taste and adds variety to pasta meals. It tends to have a grainier and nutty flavor compared to semolina based pasta. It also has a slightly different texture. The darker the color of the wheat the more full the flavor is. The nutritional values for the two pasta types are basically the same except the whole grain version is slightly higher in protein and fiber.

Fresh Lasagna Pasta

Ingredients

4 ½ cups unbleached plain flour for pasta and dusting board surface
4 very large eggs
6 oz frozen chopped spinach
½ teaspoon extra virgin olive oil

Method

Defrost the spinach and then squeeze it until it is very dry and then chop it into very fine pieces.

Lightly dust a solid wood work surface such as a chopping board. Use 3 ½ cups of flour to make a mound in the middle of the board. Form a well in the middle of the mound and then put in the eggs, spinach and olive oil.

Use a fork to beat and combine together the eggs, spinach and olive oil. As you continue beating the mixture, drag in flour from the edges of the well. The well will get bigger as more flour is incorporated in the mixture. You should try to maintain the shape of the well by dragging flour up from the base of the mound. Slowly the dough will come together as more flour is added to the mixture.

Knead the dough that forms with both of your hands. Once the dough is in a manageable form take it off the board. Scrape off the board removing any left over bits and then lightly flour it again. Place the dough ball back onto the board and continue to knead the dough with your hands until it is elastic and a bit sticky. Use plastic film to wrap the dough and leave it to rest for about half an hour at room temperature.

Once it has rested cut the dough into 3 pieces of equal size. You can now roll out each piece using the thinnest setting on the pasta machine.

Fresh Fettuccine pasta

Ingredients

3 cups unbleached plain flour, plus more for dusting
1 teaspoon salt
3 whole eggs
2 egg yolks
2 tbsp extra virgin olive oil
1 tablespoon water
Cornmeal, for dusting

Method

Mix together the flour and salt and then form it into a
mound on a lightly floured work surface or board. Make a
well in the centre of the mound and then add the whole
eggs, yolks and 1 tbsp of olive oil. Lightly beat the

contents of the well with a fork. Slowly and evenly drag in the flour from the wall of the well. Use your other hand to keep the walls of the flour mound intact. Keep adding more flour until a dough ball forms.

Knead the dough ball until it becomes smooth and elastic. Use the remaining tbsp of olive oil to brush the surface of the dough and then wrap it in plastic cling film. After allowing the pasta to rest for at least half an hour divide it into smaller portions. Shape each portion of dough into a rectangle and then pass it through a pasta rolling machine 3 times at its widest setting. Stretch and pull the dough sheet each time. Reduce the width setting on the pasta roller and pass the sheet through again another 3 times. Keep doing this until the sheet is about a quarter of an inch thick. Cut the long sheets of pasta into smaller more workable sheets and then pass them through the fettuccine cutting attachment.

Dust the fettuccine with cornmeal and then form each strand into a nest. Place on a flour dusted board to dry for around 15 minutes before using in your favorite recipe.

For variety you can add spinach to the fettuccine recipe as suggested earlier to make green pasta.

Dessert Pasta

We always think that pasta is a savory dish with tomatoes, and in the main this is true. However, the beauty of making your own pasta is that you are free to experiment and basically add whatever you want to your pasta dough. Once you have tasted sweet versions of pasta you will just want to keep coming back for more. It is fantastic served cold and can be made before you need it, as a quick dessert to be used as and when you want it. You can also experiment with lots of different toppings such as sweet fruit sauces and whipped cream. Here I have included my favorite dessert pasta recipe. Go on try it. You know you want to!

Chocolate Pasta

Ingredients

1 ¾ cup plain flour
¼ cup cocoa powder
2 tbsp granulated sugar
2 eggs
1 tbsp vegetable oil
1 tsp vanilla
Pinch of salt

Method

Put the cocoa powder, flour and salt into a large mixing bowl and combine them well using a whisk. Once they are combined well put the mixture on top of a lightly floured work surface and pile into a mound. Make a well in the middle of the mound. Put the eggs into the well and mix using a fork. As you mix them add the vegetable oil and vanilla. Drag in the flour from the inner wall of the well as you mix with the fork.

Once a soft ball of dough forms remove from the work surface, Clean the work surface and lightly flour once again. Return the dough ball to the floured surface and knead it with your hands until it becomes smooth and elastic in nature. The chocolate color should also be evenly spread throughout the dough. Wrap the dough in cling film and let it rest for at least an hour before cutting and shaping it.

Use a pasta machine to roll out the dough into sheets and then use the cutting attachment to form into the shape of pasta that you require. You can also hand shape it as described in the later chapter in this book.

As this pasta is for the dessert table you should cook it in unsalted water. Boil the pasta for about 3 minutes and then drain well. You can serve it hot with a sweet sauce or later cold after leaving to cool and chilling in the refrigerator.

You can also use this chocolate pasta to make a dessert form of tortellini. Simply make the chocolate pasta as detailed above and then form them into the classic tortellini shape with a sweet filling of your choice. Examples of fillings include chocolate and hazel nut spread, apple and cinnamon, fruit purees and so on. You can also up your game by including such things as alcoholic liqueurs such as Grand Marnier, Kirsch, Tia Maria and so on. If you want more filling than you can get into the typical tortellini then you can try making the ravioli shape instead.

Storing home made pasta

When you make fresh pasta at home it is often the case that you will have extra pasta dough left over. It is fortunate that you can store this remaining pasta for use later. If you intend to use the pasta within a few days then the refrigerator is going to be your best choice. If you want to store it for longer periods of a few months or more then you should store the pasta in the freezer.

Prepare the pasta for storage by firstly dusting the outside of the dough with a layer of flour. This flour will help to maintain the integrity of the dough, while it is being stored, by stopping moisture inside the dough from escaping and preventing extra moisture from outside getting into the pasta. You should then put plastic wrap around the pasta dough.

Put the wrapped dough inside the freezer or refrigerator. You can store the dough in the refrigerator for a couple of days and in the freezer for up to 3 months.

When you want to use the dough you need to treat it in the correct way. If the dough has been in the freezer then you should take it out in good time and put it into the refrigerator to thaw. Once thawed, or if it was in the refrigerator originally, take the dough out a few hours before you want to use it. The dough should then be left to rise up to room temperature before you use it.

Preparing pasta shapes by hand

You can cut your pasta sheets that you have made, into many different shapes but don't think that you will be able to get the intricate shapes formed in a factory where dried pasta is made. Many of these have to be made using machines with special extrusion nozzles and dies. Nevertheless, there are still quite a lot of the common pasta shapes and sizes that you can create.

Noodles

These are simply strips of pasta. The different pasta names often refer to the width of the strips. Cutting long strips of pasta accurately can be quite difficult so it is recommended that you follow these instructions when doing so.

Once you have a rolled out the sheet of pasta you should leave it to dry for about 15 minutes. After this time place it on a work surface lightly dusted with flour and sprinkle flour onto the pasta sheet as well. With the shortest side of the pasta sheet towards you begin to fold the pasta into a flattened tube shape with a width of about 3 inches. Continue folding until you have used the whole of the pasta sheet.

With the pasta roll still in front of you and using a sharp knife cut strips off the end of the rolled up pasta, rather like cutting a Swiss roll cake into slices. You can use a wooden straight edge to help you cut even strips of pasta. Cut the pasta to the size that you need. Tagliatelle is typically about ¼ inch wide and fettuccine is a little thinner than this at about 1/6 inch wide. Linguini is about 1/8 inch wide and tagliarini is around the same width and possibly a little smaller. Pappardelle should be cut to between ¾ and 1 inch in width.

Pappardelle image courtesy of Stuart Spivack

Once you have cut all of your noodles from the flattened sheet you should unroll each of them and then lay them out on a floured board or over a wooden drying rack. Leave them to dry for about 15 minutes before you cook them. This will make them firmer and also stop them sticking to each other when they are being cooked.

Tagliarini

Lasagna and Cannelloni

Cannelloni: image courtesy of Katrin Morenz

A different technique is used for other pasta types such as Lasagna. In this case, you once again start by laying the sheet of pasta on the flour dusted work surface and leave it for 15 minutes to settle. For cutting these you can use a sharp knife. If you want a wavy edge to the pasta then you can use a fluted pastry wheel. Lasagna can be cut in a number of different ways depending on the size of sheet that you want when you are cooking. Large lasagna sheets are generally up to 13 inches by about 3 inches. Lasagna rectangle shapes are usually around 6 inches by 4 inches. When deciding on a size try to make it match the baking dish that you are going to use. Use a sharp knife and a straight edge to get accurate cutting.

You should cut pasta for cannelloni in the same way. The size for this is usually around 3 inches by 4 inches. You can also make pappardelle in the same way if you don't want to use the folding method described earlier. ¾ inch wide strips should be used for this. Make sure that you keep the strips a consistent width. This is where the straight edge comes into use. Use a piece of wood or a wooden rule for this.

Farfalle

Once again start with the pasta sheet on the work surface dusted with flour. To start off with, cut squares of around 2 inches in size. To help getting consistent sizes it is a good idea to cut 2 inch strips using a straight edge first. You can then cut the individual squares out. Use a fluted pastry cutter or sharp knife depending on the type of edge that you want. The next stage is to cut the squares in half to make 2 inch by 1 inch rectangles. To form the classic farfalle butterfly shape you should pinch the middle of the long side of each of the rectangles using your thumb and a finger. Repeat the pinching process if the shape doesn't hold and springs back. Leave the completed farfalle about 15 minutes before cooking.

Farfalle and sauce

Fusille

Firstly you need to cut some 3 inch by 1/16 inch strips of pasta. The easiest way to do this is to first cut a long 3 inch strip from the pasta sheet and then cut the 1/16 inch width strips from the end of this. Once you have a lot of these strips you form the fusille by carefully wrapping them round a flour dusted wooden dowel about the size of a pencil or smaller. Once you have done this carefully slide the coiled pasta off the wooden stick. It should look like a coiled spring and you may need to press it a little so that it maintains its shape.

Garganelli

This is another kind of rolled pasta. To make these you need to cut 2 inch squares of pasta. The best method is to cut 2 inch strips from the pasta sheet and then to cut these into the 2 inch squares. To roll the garganelli you need to use a ¼ inch wooden dowel. Flour the dowel and then roll the 2 inch square of pasta onto it starting at a corner of the square. Once you have done this carefully slide the pasta off the dowel.

Orecchiette

Orecchiette are meant to look like small ears and this is reflected in the name. To make these you start with unrolled pasta. You take a piece of dough from the ball and roll it using your hands into a cylinder on a floured board. The cylinder should be long and about the thickness of a finger. If the dough becomes sticky during the rolling process sprinkle some more flour onto the board and onto your hands. Starting at one end of the rolled cylinder you need to cut off discs, of about ¼ to ½ inch in thickness. The shape of the orecchiette is formed between the thumb and the palm of your hand. Make sure that you have flour on both. Place one of the cut discs into the centre of your palm and then press your thumb into it until the disc becomes dome shaped. Remove the completed orecchiette from your palm and place on the flour dusted work surface to rest. Continue until all of the discs have been formed into orecchiette. You should let the orecchiette dry for several hours before you cook them.

Using a machine to cut and shape pasta

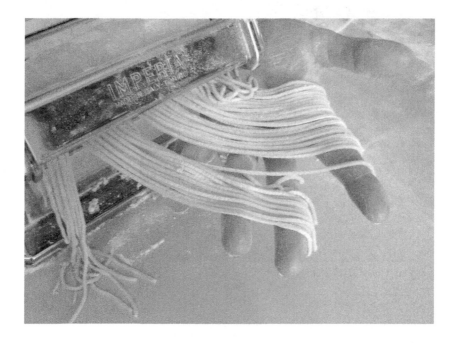

A lot of the hand rolling pasta machines, such as the Imperia models, have attachments for cutting pasta into certain shapes after the pasta has been rolled flat. The imperial has a hand cutter to size the pasta sheet correctly to be used in the attachment. On the Imperia you fit the attachment and relocate the handle to it. There are 2 slots for inserting the pasta. One of the slots cuts the pasta into tagliatelle strips and the other cuts it into spaghetti style pasta. When the handle is turned the sheet of pasta is drawn into the machine and cut to the desired width. The strips are then collected the other side of the cutter

Drying the cut pasta

Other pasta machines, whether they are electric or manual, work by pushing the pasta dough through shaped holes called dies. You can change the dies which are usually arranged in a group on a plate. Changing the plate changes the pasta shape that is formed when it is pressed through the dies. These are able to make tube like pasta such as penne and other types such as fusilli. To operate these you have to turn the handle to squeeze the pasta through the dies. Once the desired length has come through the die it has to be cut off with a sharp knife very close to the die opening. If you want a twisted form you may have to do the twisting using your fingers before leaving the pasta to dry. The dies can come in many shapes and so such things as letters of the alphabet and animal shapes like rabbits can be made.

The best uses for different pasta shapes

Listed here are the common uses for some of the popular shapes that you can make using your homemade pasta dough. In the end it is best to experiment with the things that you like.

Vermicelli

This is long and rounded pasta which isn't as thick as spaghetti. It can be used hot with light sauces or cold tossed in pasta salads

Linguine

This is long, flat and narrow pasta which is best used in hot dishes and can be used with slightly thicker sauces.

Spaghetti

Long rounded pasta of average thickness which is best used hot in tomato based sauces or baked in casseroles.

Lasagna

This is a long very wide sheet of pasta which may have straight or wavy curled edges. You can use this hot in baked and other casserole dishes.

Fusilli

Long corkscrew shaped pasta. It is very versatile pasta which can be used hot or cold and is good with most sauces, in soups or in pasta salad.

Tagliatelle

This is the same width as fettuccine and is often used in hot baked dishes and soups.

Penne

These are diagonally cut tubes that often have ridges on them. It can be used in hot soups and baked dishes with a variety of different sauces.

Penne pasta

Cannelloni

These are large long tubes which are stuffed with sauce in hot dishes.

Stuffed Pasta

Stuffed pastas aren't a modern invention and they have been enjoyed in Italy for centuries. Each region of Italy has its own variety of stuffed pasta but across the world people will recognize such pasta types as Ravioli and Tortellini.

Originally pasta stuffed with a vegetable filling was eaten on Fridays and at the time of Lent by rich people. Poorer people would eat them all of the time due to the fact that meat was so expensive. The pasta versions stuffed with meat based sauces were often made from left over's after the main Sunday lunch. In this way the meat got used up. These kinds of stuffed pasta were looked on as more of a treat than anything else. These days all varieties of stuffed past are eaten at all times.

Making your own stuffed pasta is both satisfying and interesting. Unlike buying it ready made from the supermarket you are in control of what goes into both the pasta and the filling. This is a great advantage because you can react to things that are in season and you can also make more interesting versions than the standard supermarket   ones.

You can stuff your pasta with just about any kind of vegetables, fish, meat and creamy cheeses. The best thing to do is to experiment and see what takes your fancy. Recipes for some of the most popular forms of stuffed pasta are described in the next sections of the book.

Pasta dough recipe for ravioli

Ingredients

2 cups all purpose flour, plus more for dusting
1 tsp salt
3 large eggs, plus 1 for egg wash
2 tbsp olive oil

Method using electric mixer

You should use a mixer with a dough hook to get the best results. Firstly mix the flour with the salt. Next you should add the eggs to the flour 1 at a time, while continuing to mix the ingredients. Slowly add 1 tablespoon of the olive oil and continue to combine with the flour until it forms a ball. Dust some flour on to the work surface. Next, knead and fold the dough until it becomes smooth and elastic. This process will take around ten minutes. Once you have done this brush the surface of the dough ball with the remaining olive oil. Put the ball of dough into plastic wrap and leave it to rest for around half an hour, in order to let the gluten in the dough to relax.

Method by hand

Mix together the flour and salt on a flat work surface and then shape it into a mound. Next make a well in the center of the flour and salt mixture. Put the 3 eggs and 1 tablespoon of the olive oil into this well. Lightly beat the egg and oil mixture with a fork as you slowly draw in the flour from the inside wall of the flour well, in a circular movement. You should use 1 hand for mixing with the fork and the other hand to stop the outer flour wall of the well from collapsing. Continue to slowly mix in all of the flour until it goes into a ball shape. Once the ball shape has formed you should dust some flour on to the work surface and place the dough on it. Next knead and fold the dough until it becomes smooth and elastic. This process will take around ten minutes. Once you have done this brush the surface of the dough ball with the remaining olive oil. Put the ball of dough into plastic wrap and leave it to rest for around half an hour, in order to let the gluten in the dough relax.

Rolling the Dough

You need a pasta rolling machine for the next stage. Start by cutting off half of the ball of dough. Leave the remaining half of the dough covered in the plastic wrap. Sprinkle a little flour on the work surface and place the ball of dough onto it. Press the dough with your hands into a rectangle shape and then pass it through the pasta rolling machine. You should use the widest setting and pass the dough through the machine about 3 times. As the dough comes out from the rollers you should pull and stretch it. Decrease the setting on the machine so that the gap between the rollers is smaller. Once again pass the dough through the machine about 3 times. For Ravioli the pasta has to be very thin, so you should continue to tighten up the rolling machine until the dough comes through as thin as paper. At this point you should be able to see through it. Once the rolling is complete dust the long sheets of dough formed with some flour.

Making the Ravioli Shapes

Image courtesy of fugzu

Firstly you have to make an egg wash. To do this beat an egg with a tablespoon of water. Sprinkle the work surface and sheet of dough with flour. Put the long sheet of pasta on the dusted work surface and then brush the top surface with the egg wash. This will act as the glue when putting ravioli shapes together. Use a tablespoon to place ravioli filling on half of the pasta sheet. Each tablespoon of filling should be placed about 2 inches apart from each other. You should then take the other half of the pasta sheet and fold it over the filled area. This is rather like folding a blanket. Once you have done this you need to use your fingers to carefully press out any air that is trapped in bubbles around each mound of filling. Get a sharp knife and carefully cut the mounds and surrounding pasta into squares. You can use a fluted pastry wheel if you want a wavy edge to the ravioli. Press the edges of each square of pasta with your fingers to ensure that the glue makes a good seal around the mound of filling. Dust the formed ravioli and put them on a flour dusted surface to prevent them sticking, while you deal with rest of the pasta that you intend to make. The Ravioli are now ready for cooking, which you do in the normal way using boiling water.

Tortellini with a spinach and ricotta filling

Tortellinis are a form of small stuffed pasta shapes. There are various fillings that you can make to create very interesting eating experiences. They are delicious on their own with a simple cheese garnish or can be served with various sauces or even in soups.

Ingredients

Dough
4 cups plain Flour
1 tsp Salt
3 eggs
4 tbsp Cold Water

Spinach Ricotta Filling
1 cup chopped and cooked spinach,
½ cup Ricotta cheese
¼ cup grated Parmesan cheese
3 tbsp dry bread crumbs
Salt
Pepper, to taste

Method

Making the dough

Sift the flour and then add it together with the salt to a large mixing bowl. Mix them together with a metal whisk to combine them. While still in the bowl make a well in the middle of the flour mixture and then add the eggs and water. Use a fork to mix the liquids together and gradually drag the flour into the centre. Keep mixing until a ball of dough is formed. You can add more flour or water to get the right consistency for the dough.

Lightly flour a work surface and then put the ball of dough onto it. Knead the dough until it is smooth and elastic. Cover the dough with plastic wrap and leave to rest for between 20 and 30 minutes.

Making the filling

Drain the cooked spinach thoroughly. Mix the spinach with the Ricotta, Parmesan and bread crumbs and then season with salt and pepper to taste. Make sure all the ingredients are well combined.

Making the Tortellini

Cut the dough in half and then roll out each piece until it forms a sheet about 1/8 of an inch thick. Use a cutter to stamp out circles that are 1 ½ inch in diameter. Put half a teaspoon of the filling in the center of each pasta circle. Fold each circle in half and then firmly press the edges together to seal the filling in. Next pull the ends of the half circle together so that you have a ring. This should make the tortellini look a little like a belly button or navel.

To cook them first prepare a large pot of lightly salted boiling water. Drop the tortellini into the boiling water and allow them to cook for about 6 minutes. They will rise to the surface of the boiling water when they are cooked. Use a slotted spoon to remove them from the boiling water and serve with either a sauce or simply grated Parmesan and melted butter.

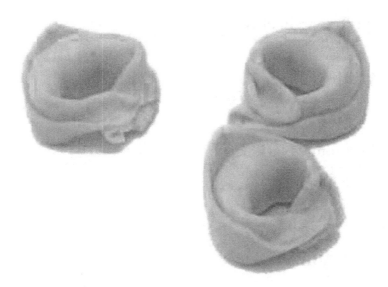

Tortellini: image courtesy of Gyfis

Agnolotti stuffed with beef and spinach

Agnolotti are a little bit like ravioli but originate from a different region of Italy. This particular kind of stuffed pasta is square in shape and about 1 inch in size. Agnolotti are typically stuffed with meats but cheeses and vegetables are often used these days too. They can be served with a sauce but are equally at home when used in soups.

Ingredients

Pasta dough
2 ¼ cups plain flour
3 eggs
¾ tsp salt
1 tbsp extra virgin olive oil
1 tbsp warm water

Beef filling
2 tbsp extra virgin olive oil
12 oz beef chuck steak
Salt
Freshly ground black pepper
1 small onion
2 minced garlic cloves
1 sprig of rosemary
½ cup chicken broth

Spinach filling
1 tbsp butter
1 tbsp olive oil
12 ounces fresh spinach
Salt
Freshly ground black pepper
1 egg
Pinch of grated nutmeg
1/3 cup grated Parmesan cheese

Agnolotti sauce
6 oz of butter
8 sage leaves
Parmesan cheese

Method

Making the dough

Lightly flour a work surface or board. Put the flour in a pile on the work surface and make a well in the middle. Put the eggs into the well together with the salt, olive oil and warm water.

Beat the mixture in the well with a fork and slowly drag in and incorporate the flour from the sides of the well. Keep beating until the dough gets hard to mix and also sticky as well. At this point use your hands to shape the dough into a ball.

Clean off the work surface and lightly flour it once again. Place the dough ball onto the floured surface and knead it until it becomes smooth and elastic. Wrap the dough in plastic wrap and leave to rest for at least 30 minutes before cutting and shaping.

Making the beef and spinach filling

You will need to start cooking the beef well before you plan to make up the stuffed agnolotti because it takes a long time to prepare.

Cut the beef up into 1 inch cubes and then season with salt and pepper. Peel and slice the onion. Cook the beef in a saucepan with the olive oil over a medium heat. Once the meat has browned on its surfaces add the onion, rosemary, garlic and chicken broth to the pan. Bring the mixture to boiling and then reduce the heat and simmer for about 60 minutes. Once the meat is tender turn off the heat and put to one side to cool. You will need both the beef and the cooking juices for the next stage of preparation.

Coarsely chop the spinach and then add it to a large frying pan containing the melted butter and olive oil over a medium heat. Season with salt and pepper and cook the spinach until it becomes wilted and is nice and tender. Put the cooked spinach into a colander and leave it to cool and drain.

Once the beef is cool, remove it from the cooking juices and chop it up into small pieces with a knife on a chopping board. Transfer the chopped beef to a large bowl and then add it back the cooking juices. Stir in the cooked spinach and then add the egg, Parmesan cheese and nutmeg. Stir once again and season to taste with salt and pepper.

Preparing the agnolotti

Divide the pasta dough up into four pieces and then roll each through a pasta machine until it is nice and thin. At this point the sheet of pasta formed will be about twelve inches in length and about 4 inches in width. Place each sheet of pasta in turn onto a floured work surface to prepare the agnolotti. Starting 1 inch from the bottom and 1 inch from the side put 1 tbsp of the beef and spinach filling at 2 inch intervals along the length of the pasta sheet. Use a pastry brush to moisten the long edge of the pasta sheet and between the heaps of filling. Fold the empty side of the pasta over the fillings to meet the opposite long edge. Press the long edges of the pasta together to seal them. Pinch the dough between the mounds of filling to seal these areas too. Next use a pastry wheel between the mounds of filling to separate out the individual agnolotti. Place the completed agnolotti onto a floured surface to rest.

Making the agnolotti sauce

Melt the butter in a large frying pan set on a low heat. Next add the sage leaves to the melted butter. The butter will absorb the flavor from the sage leaves.

Cooking the agnolotti

Prepare a large pot of lightly salted water and bring to the boil. Put the agnolotti in batches of no more than 20 into the boiling water and cook for around 4 minutes. Stir the agnolotti every now and then to prevent them from sticking. Take the agnolotti from the pan and drain the water off them. Straight away put them into the pan with the butter sauce and make sure that they are well coated with it. Put the agnolotti on to individual plates and serve with a garnish of grated parmesan cheese.

Cappelletti stuffed with prosciutto, sausage and chicken

This form of stuffed pasta has the shape of a little hat and this is what the name Cappelletti actually means. It is usually served with a broth but can be also used with sauces as well.

Ingredients

3 ½ oz sliced prosciutto
3 ½ oz mortadella sausage
5 oz chicken breast
2 tbsp butter
½ medium onion
1 cup grated Parmigianino
½ cup white wine
1 egg
Salt
Pepper
Grated nutmeg
Fresh pasta

Method

To make the filling first finely chop the onion and cut up the chicken breast into 1 inch pieces. Melt the butter in a frying pan on a medium heat. Put the chicken and onion into the pan and fry while stirring until the onion is softened and chicken is cooked and no longer pink. Add the wine and then increase the heat. Continue to cook until most of the wine has gone. Take the pan from the heat and put to one side to cool.

Chop the prosciutto and mortadella sausage into small pieces and put it into a food processor. Add the cooled chicken from the pan and then run the food processor until it becomes smooth. Add half a cup of Parmigianino and run the food processor once again to combine it all together. Add salt and pepper seasoning to taste and then crack the egg into the processor bowl. Use the pulse feature of the processor until the mixture is well blended. Add some grated nutmeg to taste. Transfer the blended mixture to a bowl, cover and leave to rest in the refrigerator for about 30 minutes.

Now it is time to prepare the pasta. Make a pasta mix similar to that used for the Ravioli or Tortellini as described above. Use a pasta machine to roll out the pasta until flat sheets are formed that will go through on the thinnest setting of the machine.

Use a sharp knife to cut the sheets of pasta into squares that are about 1 ½ inches in size. Use a spoon to place a small amount of filling in the centre of each pasta square. Fold each pasta square so that it makes a triangle shape and press the edges together. Grasp the 2 corners along the long edge of the triangle, bring them together and press to fix them in place. The remaining corner should be bent back to give the classic cappelletti shape.

Fresh pasta dough meal recipes

Here you will find some example recipes for each of the pasta types described above. You can start with these and then go on to experiment yourself with the various shapes of pasta and the meals that you can use them in.

Lemon and black pepper linguine seafood

Ingredients

8 oz fresh lemon and black pepper linguine
4 tbsp extra virgin olive oil
2 tbsp chopped garlic
1 tbsp lemon pepper
1 pound peeled and deveined medium sized shrimp
½ cup grated Parmesan cheese
Green salad
Lemon wedges

Method

Put the linguine into a large pot of lightly salted boiling water and cook until the pasta is al dente. Once it is cooked drain the water from the pasta.

Put the olive oil into a large frying pan and place it on the hob set to a medium heat. Add the chopped garlic, lemon pepper and shrimp and cook until the shrimp turns to a nice pink color. Once cooked add the shrimp to the pasta and toss it together with the Parmesan cheese. Serve with a green salad garnish and lemon wedges.

Orecchiette carbonara

Image courtesy of Foodista

Ingredients

Lightly salted water
3 oz thick sliced smoked bacon
4 oz pancetta
1 tbsp extra virgin olive oil
1 large onion
2 cloves garlic
1 ½ cups fresh or frozen peas
2 tsp thyme leaves
3 eggs
6 egg yolks
1 ¾ cups grated Parmigiano Reggiano cheese
1 lb fresh orecchiette
Freshly ground black pepper
20 small spinach leaves
½ lemon
2 tbsp coarsely chopped fresh parsley

Method

Chop the bacon into cubes that are about ¼ inch in size. Chop the pancetta into ¼ inch sized chunks. Chop the onion and the garlic.

Cook the cubes of bacon in the olive oil in a large frying pan placed on a medium to low heat. Continue to cook the bacon until it has lost most of its fat and has browned nicely. Drain off most of the bacon fat from the pan but leave about a tbsp in there for further cooking. Leave the bacon in the pan and then add the onion and the garlic. Continue to cook until the onion turns translucent. Next add the thyme and the peas. Stir these in and then cook for another few minutes.

Gently whisk the eggs and egg yolks together with the cheese in a large bowl and save for use later.

Put the pasta into a large pot of lightly salted boiling water and cook until the pasta is al dente. Once it is cooked drain the water from the pasta. Start to heat the bacon in the pan once again. Add the pasta to the frying pan with the bacon. Season with the freshly ground black pepper and then stir the pasta gently with the bacon mixture in the pan

Pour in the egg and cheese mixture and then quickly and gently mix everything together. The eggs should start to cook in the pan and as they do so they will coat the pasta and form a smooth sauce. Next add the spinach leaves and gently mix once again. Squeeze in the lemon juice to taste and check the seasoning. The pasta is now ready to serve and you should place it in bowls and garnish with the freshly chopped parsley.

Tagliatelle with Chicken and mushroom

Ingredients

3 chicken breasts
1 large onion
2 cups chopped mushrooms
2 cups single cream
160g fresh tagliatelle
2 tbsp extra virgin olive oil
1 ½ tsp salt
1 tbsp freshly ground black pepper

Method

Dice the chicken breasts and chop the onions.

Put the olive oil into a pan on a medium heat and then add the chopped onions. Fry the onions and then after a couple of minutes add the diced chicken to the pan. Continue cooking until the chicken turns from pink to white on all surfaces.

Put the mushrooms into the pan and cook for another couple of minutes. Next add the cream followed by the salt and pepper seasoning. Make sure that you turn the heat down to low and stir often so that the creamy mixture only just simmers.

Put the tagliatelle into a large pot of lightly salted boiling water and cook until the pasta is al dente. Once it is cooked drain the water from the pasta. Add the pasta to the creamy sauce and make sure it is well covered before serving.

Fettuccine Alfredo

Ingredients

1 pint heavy cream
½ cup softened unsalted butter
1 cup grated Parmigiano Reggiano
Freshly ground black pepper
Chopped fresh flat leaf parsley, for garnish

Method

Put the heavy cream in a saucepan and heat it on a low to medium setting. Add the butter to the pan and then whisk it gently to help it melt into the cream. Add the grated Parmigiano Reggiano and stir the mixture to combine it with the cream and butter. Season the mixture to taste with the freshly ground black pepper.

Cook the fresh fettuccine pasta in a large pot of boiling salted water for about 3 minutes. Immediately drain the pasta and add it to the pan with the cream and cheese mixture. Toss the fettuccine pasta so that it becomes coated with the Alfredo sauce. Once this is done serve in individual bowls with a garnish of chopped parsley and grated Parmigiano Reggiano.

Baked tagliarini with beef

Ingredients

2 tbsp extra virgin olive oil
1 green pepper
1 lb ground beef
½ lb strong cheddar cheese
1 clove minced garlic
1 minced small onion
½ cup sliced olives
¼ cup water
4 oz fresh tagliarini
12 oz can whole kernel corn
1 lb can tomatoes
½ tsp salt
¼ tsp freshly ground black pepper

Method

Chop the green pepper and shred the Cheddar cheese.

Put the tagliarini into a large pot of lightly salted boiling water and cook until the pasta is al dente. Once it is cooked drain the water from the pasta.

Heat the olive oil in a large pan on a medium heat. Add the ground beef and the chopped green pepper. Cook the mixture while stirring until all of the red color of the ground beef has gone. Next stir in the garlic, onion, Cheddar cheese and olives. Once these ingredients are combined stir in the water, cooked tagliarini, corn, tomatoes, salt and black pepper.

Pour and spoon the combined mixture into a well greased casserole dish. Bake the mixture in a preheated oven set to 180C for about 45 minutes.

Pappardelle with Spinach and ricotta cheese

Ingredients

12 oz fresh pappardelle
2 tbsp extra virgin olive oil
4 spring onions
1 tbsp chopped sage
10 oz baby spinach
2 tbsp butter
1 cup ricotta cheese
¼ cup grated Parmigiano-Reggiano cheese
Salt and freshly ground black pepper
Grated Parmigiano and chopped parsley garnish

Method

Thinly slice the spring onions and cut the butter into cubes.

Put the pappardelle into a large pot of lightly salted boiling water and cook until the pasta is al dente. Once it is cooked drain the water from the pasta. Save the cooking water for use later in making the sauce.

Put the olive oil into a large frying pan and set on a high heat. Put the sage and spring onions into the pan and cook until they are just browned. Add the spinach to the pan and continue to cook while stirring the mixture until the spinach has wilted.

Put the cooked pappardelle, ricotta cheese and butter into the pan and toss the mixture to cover the pasta. Put 2/3 of a cup of the saved pasta cooking water into the pan and then add the Parmigiano cheese. Season the mixture well with the salt and black pepper. Reduce the heat to low and continue to cook and toss the mixture until the sauce becomes creamy and thick. If the sauce becomes too thick add extra cooking water until the consistency is right.

Serve the pappardelle straight away in bowls with a garnish of grated Parmigiano and chopped parsley.

Lasagna with a Bolognese sauce

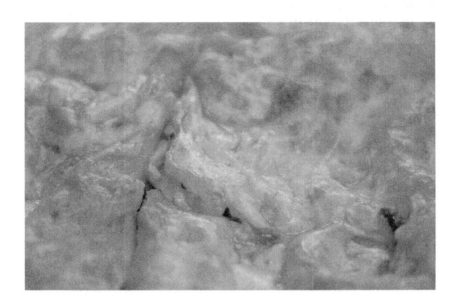

Ingredients

For the pasta
Fresh Lasagna pasta
2 tbsp salt
Cold water
8 ounces Parmigiano Reggiano

For the Bolognese Sauce
¼ cup extra virgin olive oil
4 tbsp butter
2 medium onions
4 stalks celery
1 carrot
5 cloves garlic

1 lb ground veal
1 lb ground pork
½ lb ground beef
¼ lb minced pancetta
½ cup milk
16 oz can crushed tomatoes
1 cup dry white wine
1 cup beef broth
Salt and pepper

For the béchamel sauce
5 tbsp butter
4 tbsp flour
3 cups milk
1 tsp salt
½ tsp freshly grated nutmeg

Method

Preparing the pasta:
Make the fresh lasagna pasta as described in the previous section of the book.

Put about 12 pints of water into a large pot and then add the 2 tbsp of salt. Heat the salted water until it is boiling. Put the cold water in a bowl near to the pot with the boiling water. Take the prepared fresh pasta and use a sharp knife to cut it into squares that are about five inch in size. Take the pasta squares and drop them into the boiling water. Cook the pasta for about a minute. This should make it tender. Remove the pasta from the boiling water and drain it well. Place immediately into the cold water in the bowl to cool. Once the pasta is cool drain it once again and leave to one side for use later on.

Preparing the Bolognese sauce
Finely chop the onions and celery. Scrape the carrots and then finely chop these too. Slice the garlic cloves.

Heat the olive oil and butter in a large saucepan on a medium heat. Add the onions, carrot and garlic the pan and cook until the onions become transparent. Increase the heat to high and then mix in the veal, beef, pancetta and pork. Cook the meats while stirring until they are nicely browned. Put the milk into the pan and reduce the heat to a simmer. Continue cooking until the mixture is just about dry. Next add the tomatoes and continue to simmer for about a quarter of an hour. Mix in the beef broth and the white wine and bring the mixture to the boil followed by simmering for about 2 hours. After cooking season the sauce with the salt and pepper.

Preparing the béchamel sauce
Heat the butter in a saucepan until it melts. Next, pour in the flour and stir until you have a smooth mixture. Continue to cook the mixture until it becomes lightly browned.

In another pan heat the milk and then just before it is boiling pour it into the pan with the butter and flour mixture. Cook the sauce for about another 10 minutes and then add seasoning and ground nutmeg. Leave to one side until needed for putting the Lasagna together.

Cooking the lasagna
In a suitable baking pan or dish start to put the lasagna together. Start with a layer of the Bolognese sauce followed by a sprinkling of the grated Parmigiano cheese and then the cooked pasta, followed by a layer of the béchamel sauce. Start a new layer with more Bolognese sauce and continue adding layers until the ingredients are used up. You should make sure that the top layer of the lasagna is made up of a layer of pasta covered with a final layer of béchamel sauce. Finally sprinkle Parmigiano on the top and then bake in a preheated oven set to 190C for about an hour or until the lasagna is bubbling and the

edges are nice and golden brown. After cooking take the lasagna from the oven and allow it to cool for about 15 minutes. Sprinkle the top with some more Parmigiano and serve while hot.

Cannelloni with spinach and ricotta cheese

Ingredients

1 ¾ cups tomato passatta
600g ricotta cheese
250g frozen spinach
2 tbsp chopped flat leaf parsley
2 tbsp chopped basil
2/3 cup grated parmesan cheese
Salt and freshly ground black pepper
6 fresh cannelloni sheets
1 cup grated mozzarella
Green salad

Method

Thaw and chop the spinach.

Take an oven proof dish that is about 20cm by 30 cm and 4cm deep. Lightly grease the dish and then pour in 1 cup of the passatta. Use a spoon or knife to spread the passatta evenly over the bottom of the dish.

Get a big mixing bowl and then add the spinach, ricotta, parsley, basil, 1/3 cup of grated parmesan, salt and pepper. Mix the ingredients until they are well combined.

Take the fresh cannelloni sheets and one by one place them on a lightly floured board. Into each one put about a third of a cup of the ricotta spinach mixture and then roll up each cannelloni sheet into a tube. You should be able to fill about eight cannelloni with the mixture.

Place the filled cannelloni side by side in the dish on top of the passatta in the base. Spoon the remaining ¾ cup of passatta over the cannelloni. Sprinkle the grated mozzarella and the remaining 1/3 cup of parmesan over the top and then bake in a preheated oven set to 190C for about 30 minutes or until the cheese topping is golden brown. Serve the cooked cannelloni with the green salad.

Farfalle and Prosciutto salad

Ingredients

1 lb fresh farfalle pasta
40z prosciutto
12 oz cherry tomatoes
1 bunch fresh basil
2 tsp minced garlic
4 oz extra virgin olive oil
1 ½ oz balsamic vinegar
1 cup finely grated parmesan cheese
Sea salt
Freshly ground black pepper

Method

Put the farfalle into a large pot of lightly salted boiling water and cook until the pasta is al dente. Once it is cooked drain the water from the pasta. Save the cooking water for use later in making the sauce.

Cut the cherry tomatoes in half. Dice the prosciutto. Cut the basil julienne style until you have about ½ a cup.

Put a tbsp olive oil and the minced garlic into a pan and fry gently on a low heat until it becomes a golden brown color. Next add the prosciutto and the tomatoes to the pan and toss the mixture well to combine them. Take the pan away from the heat and put to one side for use later.

Put the balsamic vinegar into a small bowl and then add the rest of the olive oil. Whisk the contents of the bowl until they form an emulsion suitable as a salad dressing.

Put the cooked farfalle pasta into a large mixing bowl and then add the tomato and prosciutto mixture from the pan. Toss the pasta well.

Next add ¼ cup of the saved pasta cooking water followed by the balsamic salad dressing. Season to taste with the sea salt and freshly ground black pepper. Gently mix in half of the grated parmesan cheese and season again if needed.

On serving the pasta salad, garnish it with the remaining grated parmesan cheese.

Fusilli with Portobello mushroom, olives and ricotta

Ingredients

2 tbsp olive oil
1 ½ oz Portobello mushroom
1 garlic clove

12 oz pitted green olives
9 oz heavy cream
¼ bunch mint
¼ bunch flat leaf parsley
14 oz fusilli pasta
3 ½ fresh ricotta
3 ½ Parmesan cheese
Sea salt
Freshly ground black pepper
Garnish
2 red chilies
1 lemon
Extra virgin olive oil

Method

Finely chop the Portobello mushroom. Chop the garlic clove and the olives. Remove the leaves from the mint and then chop them. Crumble the ricotta cheese and grate the Parmesan. Chop the chilies. Chop the parsley

Put the olive oil into a large heavy skillet and cook the mushrooms over a medium heat until they have released their juices. Next add the olives and garlic and continue cooking until the liquid has gone. Add the cream and then gently simmer the mixture until the amount of cream has reduced to a half of that started with. Sprinkle in half of the chopped mint and parsley.

Put the fusilli into a large pot of lightly salted boiling water and cook until the pasta is al dente. Once it is cooked drain the water from the pasta. Add the pasta to the mushroom and olive mixture and toss to combine. Stir in the Parmesan can ricotta cheese. Season the pasta to taste with the salt and black pepper.

When you are ready to serve put it into bowls and garnish with the chopped chilies and the remaining chopped herbs. Squeeze some of the lemon juice on the top of each bowl and add a drizzle of olive oil

Garganelli with Asparagus and Parmigiano Reggiano

Ingredients

8 oz fresh garganelli pasta
2 tbsp extra virgin olive oil
2 ½ cups 1 inch slices of asparagus
1 cup chicken broth
1 tbsp grated lemon rind
1 minced garlic clove
¼ cup grated Parmigiano Reggiano
½ tsp sea salt
½ tsp freshly ground black pepper
2 tbsp shaved Parmigiano Reggiano

Method

Put the garganelli into a large pot of lightly salted boiling water and cook until the pasta is al dente. Once it is cooked drain the water from the pasta.

Put the olive oil into a large frying pan and put on a medium heat. Put the sliced asparagus into the oil and cook while stirring every now and then until it is tender. Remove the asparagus from the pan and put to one side. Next, put the broth, lemon rind and garlic into the pan and continue to cook until the liquid has reduced and there is only about half a cup left in the pan. Put the asparagus slices back into the pan and then add the pasta, grated Parmigiano Reggiano, salt and black pepper. Toss the pasta so that it becomes coated with the sauce. Serve in pasta bowls and garnish with the shaved Parmigiano Reggiano.

Spaghetti Aglio e Olio

Ingredients

1 lb fresh spaghetti
6 cloves garlic, thinly sliced
½ cup extra virgin olive oil
¼ teaspoon red pepper flakes
Salt
Freshly ground black pepper
¼ cup chopped fresh Italian parsley
1 cup finely grated Parmigiano Reggiano cheese

Method

Put the spaghetti into a large pot of lightly salted boiling water. Cook the spaghetti and stir every now and then until it is al dente. Drain the pasta and then put it into a pasta bowl.

Put the garlic and olive oil into a frying pan and then cook on a medium heat so that the garlic slowly toasts. Lower the heat once the olive oil starts to bubble and continue to cook the garlic. The key to perfection is to toast the garlic slices slowly to a golden brown in the olive oil. You will find that if the garlic is too light then you won't get the full flavor and yet if it is too dark then the flavor becomes bitter. You should practice getting it right. Once the garlic is cooked remove the pan from the heat.

Stir the red pepper flakes, black pepper and salt into the pasta to taste. Next, pour in the olive oil and add the cooked garlic. Sprinkle on the parsley and ½ cup of the Parmigiano Reggiano cheese. Stir the pasta until everything is combined.

Serve the pasta in bowls and garnish each portion with the remaining ½ cup of the Parmigiano Reggiano cheese.

Vermicelli with anchovy sauce

Ingredients

2 garlic cloves
1 ½ cups parsley leaves
1 onion
4 anchovy fillets
1/3 cup pitted green olives
2 tsp capers
½ tsp salt
¼ tsp black pepper
½ cup extra virgin olive oil
1 tsp extra virgin olive oil
1 lb vermicelli

Method

Slice the onion. Rinse and pat dry the anchovy fillets.

Add the garlic, parsley, sliced onion, anchovies, olives, capers and black pepper to a food processor. Process the ingredients until they are finely chopped. Add the ½ cup of olive oil and continue to process the mixture until the oil is well combined with the other ingredients.

Put the vermicelli into a large pot of lightly salted boiling water and cook until the pasta is al dente. Once it is cooked, drain well using a colander. Once drained, return the vermicelli to the pot and toss with the 1 tsp of olive oil.

Put the pasta into a large serving bowl. Pour the anchovy sauce over the pasta and then toss well to coat the vermicelli. Serve the pasta straight away.

Penne with beef sauce

Ingredients

8 oz fresh penne pasta
2 tbsp olive oil
2 cups chopped onion
2 chopped cloves garlic
1 tsp Italian seasoning
Pinch of red pepper flakes
½ tsp fresh thyme
Salt
Freshly ground black pepper
1 lb ground beef
3 fresh chopped basil leaves
2 ½ cups canned peeled tomatoes
1 tsp sugar
1 tbsp chopped fresh parsley

Method

Put the penne into a large pot of lightly salted boiling water and cook until the pasta is al dente. Once it is cooked drain the water from the pasta.

Put the olive oil into a large frying pan and put on a medium heat. Cook the chopped onion, Italian seasoning and red pepper flakes while stirring every now and then until the onions become soft. Next, put in the garlic, thyme, salt and pepper seasoning. Cook for a couple of minutes and then remove from the heat and put to one side.

Heat a large saucepan on a high heat and once the pan is hot throw in small chunks of the ground beef. Let the chunks of beef brown on once side and then use a spatula to flip them over to brown the other sides

Transfer the cooked meat from the saucepan to the frying pan with the onions using a slotted spoon. Add the tomatoes, basil and sugar and then heat until simmering and continue to cook for about 15 minutes. Season the sauce with salt and pepper and then stir in the cooked penne pasta. Serve straight away in bowls with a garnish of sprinkled chopped parsley.

Tortellini and Italian sausage soup

Ingredients

3 ½ oz link sweet Italian sausage
1 cup chopped onions
2 minced cloves garlic

5 cups beef stock
1/3 cup water
½ cup red wine
4 tomatoes
1 cup chopped carrots
½ teaspoon dried basil
½ teaspoon dried oregano
1 cup Italian tomato sauce
1 zucchini
8 oz fresh cheese and spinach tortellini
1 green bell pepper
1 tbsp chopped fresh parsley
2 tbsp grated Parmesan cheese for topping

Method

Make the cheese and spinach tortellini as described in the previous section.

Peel and remove the seeds from the tomatoes and then chop them. Chop the zucchini and the bell pepper. Remove the casing from the sausage.

Brown the sausage meat well in a large saucepan on a medium to high heat setting. Once it is browned drain off most of the fat leaving only about a tbsp of it in the pan. Add the garlic and onions to the pan and then cook for about 6 minutes.

Put the water, beef stock, wine, tomatoes, basil, carrots, oregano and tomato sauce into the pot with the cooked sausage meat. Heat the pan until the mixture is boiling and then reduce the heat until it is simmering. Continue to simmer the mixture for about half an hour. If fat collects on the surface of the liquid skim it off.

Put the tortellini, zucchini, bell pepper and parsley into the pan and then cook for about a further 10 minutes until the tortellini is nice and tender. Put the soup into bowls and serve with a garnish of grated Parmesan cheese.

Cappelletti in chicken broth

Ingredients

Freshly made Cappelletti
2 four pound chickens
2 carrots
2 celery stalks
1 large white onion
7 pints cold water
1 tsp sea salt
4 oz Parmigiano Reggiano cheese rind
Grated Parmigiano for garnish

Method

Make the Cappelletti as described in the previous section. Cut the chicken into 6 pieces. Cut each carrot and each celery stalk into thirds. Peel the onion and then cut into thirds.

Put the chicken, celery, carrots and onion into a large pot and then add the water and the salt. Heat the mixture until it is boiling and then reduce the heat until it is simmering. Continue to cook the broth for 2 hours and skim off any foam and fat that comes to the surface. Put in the cheese rinds and simmer for a further hour.

Once it is cooked pour the mixture through a large sieve made of fine mesh. Press the solids hard into the sieve and then remove and discard. Season the broth with extra salt if needed.

Replace the broth into the pot and add the fresh cappelletti. Heat the mixture until boiling and then simmer for about 10 minutes. Spoon the mixture into serving bowls and garnish with Parmigiano.

Conclusion

Making your own pasta dough isn't as difficult as you perhaps thought. There is also a mental satisfaction from producing food from the very basic ingredients and using your own physical efforts. Pasta making machines can help to reduce the work involved in making your own pasta. You can get machines to do all of the work and there are plenty of them on the market these days. You can also get machines that will help with specific aspects of pasta making such as rolling the pasta and cutting simple shapes. Which ever method, you choose to make your pasta; you should see that there are almost limitless variations that can be made in the final results.

Once you get a taste for making your own pasta there suddenly comes the need to experiment more to see what other exciting ideas you can come up with. Making pasta is an art and not a science. You can, therefore, vary the ingredients in the pasta dough mix to see what happens.

The recipes given here are not set in stone, and it is up to you to put your own stamp on them. You can change the ingredients in terms of exactly what they are and the amounts used. You can even come up with your own pasta shapes to make truly unique dishes that are particular to you. Whatever you decide to do, I hope that this book has given you the inspiration to carry on making your own pasta so that it becomes a natural part of your day to day cooking routine.

About the Author

Elisabetta Parisi knows about pasta and it is her passion for pasta over the year that has resulted in the production of this book. Pasta is in her blood and in her genes. In Italy pasta is a part of life and this shows in the energy and skill that Elisabetta puts into her cooking.

Good pasta means starting with the right ingredients and then making everything from scratch. Add to this the know how passed down through generations and you have the contents of this book.

If you are new to homemade pasta then this is the perfect place to start. You may think that making pasta is hard but this book soon puts your mind at rest so that you can get on with the cooking. It contains basic information on flours that you can use for pasta; the different ways of mixing and rolling the dough; how to shape the pasta and of course how to cook it.

The first version of this book released on Kindle was a much shorter production which concentrated on the accurate making of a limited number of pasta doughs. This book was praised for being short, sweet and to the point. Many people bought the book and it proved to be very popular in the Italian section where it quickly became number 1 in the top 100 books sold. Based on this success, Elisabetta has reviewed and extended the material in the original book so that it contains far more pasta dough ideas including how to produce a variety of stuffed pasta and dessert pasta. This then resulted in the version of the book currently published as a paperback and on Kindle as well.

Elisabetta is skilled in the cooking of a variety of other Italian dishes as well as a number of other European styles and this has resulted in the production of a number of other Kindle releases that you may be interested in:

Panini Recipes

Elisabetta Parisi

The Panini classic recipe depends on the Panini bread that you use with a Panini sandwich so why not bake your own and use it with the delicious Panini sandwich recipes including chicken Panini recipes given here.

Panini Recipes can be exciting as well as quick. You are really missing out if you don't have this Italian inspired food at home. You can put just about anything into a panini so long as it is cooked first. The taste of a panini is influenced by the quality of the bread that you use. You can buy Italian bread but why not go that extra step and make some yourself. This book contains some easy recipes for panini bread including Ciabatta and Focaccia. You can make these quickly and improve your panini experience greatly. Try your new homemade panini bread with some of the exciting panini recipes in this book.

Penne Pasta Recipes

Penne pasta includes the popular recipes of Penne alla vodka, Penne arrabiata, Penne carbonara and baked Penne

Elisabetta Parisi

Penne Pasta Recipes for great meals using this very versatile pasta shape. Penne is fantastic with sauces, in soups and with salads. Learn how to cook Penne so that it can absorb and hold the sauces you add to it. Make the basic Marinara sauce and you can use this as the basis for a lot of other recipes and build upon its flavors to produce many exciting dishes including Penne alla Vodka and Penne Carbonara. Feel the spice in Penne Arrabiatta and cook with Italian sausage for extra flavor. Learn the recipes in this book and you will be able to produce a huge variety of pasta dishes rather than the inevitable Spag Bol which seems to turn up on the menu every week.

Bruschetta Recipe

Bruschetta recipes start with Bruschetta bread and then tomato Bruschetta with basil going on to easy Bruschetta recipe with different Bruschetta toppings

Elisabetta Parisi

Bruschetta Recipe explains how to get started with these very tasty Italian based appetizers and snacks. Technique and ingredients are very important when it comes to producing the basic Bruschetta. There are a number of ways to prepare and cook Bruschetta and these are explained in this book. There are lots of recipes for exciting toppings employing different breads and different ways of cooking Bruschetta. You can make small tasty snacks as part of a finger buffet or larger ones that you can uses as a full meal with and eat with a knife and fork. Bruschetta are the essential taste of the Italian summer with fresh ripe tomatoes and basil from the garden. What more could you want?

Tapas Recipes

Covers what are tapas and includes Spanish tapas recipes to make lots of tapas dishes so that you can build your own tapas menu based on Spanish tapas and other world tapas ideas

Elisabetta Parisi

Tapas Recipes has lots of tasty tapas foods for you to make at home. Tapas food is becoming more popular all of the time with tapas bars opening up across the world and big supermarkets stocking their own tapas lines. You can make your own tapas out of fresh ingredients, enjoy them with some Spanish wine and relive those glorious summer holiday times. Tapas are great as snacks and even better with wine or beer. They are also a great alternative to the usual sausage rolls and paste sandwiches of a typical buffet spread. Enjoy them on your own and contemplate the world or entertain with them it is your choice! Each recipe is easy to follow with no strange ingredients that are hard to get. Go on, have a change and make some tapas.

Mushroom Recipes

For Portobello mushroom recipes, mushroom soup recipes, stuffed mushroom recipes, chicken and mushroom recipes and stuffed Portabella mushroom recipes

Elisabetta Parisi

Mushrooms are one of the most versatile foods that there is. They can be used as an accent to a meal, a tasty addition or as the main event. Mushrooms are full of different tastes and flavors depending on the variety you choose and the age of the mushroom. Small mushrooms are white with a delicate flavor and large Portobello mushrooms have a full on nutty flavor. Portobello mushrooms can even be used as a substitute for steak when it comes to steak and chips. They are also great in stews and soups. All types of mushroom can add body to soups and stews and as special treats can be stuffed with interesting ingredients and baked. Mushrooms are also a healthy choice, being packed with vitamins and minerals but virtually fat and carbohydrate free. This can be a real bonus for anybody on a diet. Mushrooms can also make you feel full and less likely to snack between meals. Get your mushroom head on a try my selection of really tasty dishes using mushrooms. You can try soups, casseroles, stir fries and lots of stuffed versions with tasty cheeses and even sausage meats. Once you get into mushrooms it can become a passion and you can take it further by using more exotic varieties of cultivated mushrooms or even become and expert and go searching for the wild ones. Get into mushrooms and find out what you are missing!

Ground Turkey Recipes

Recipes for ground turkey include lots of healthy ground turkey recipes and recipes with ground turkey that are tasty and filling such as ground turkey casserole recipes. Find the ultimate ground turkey recipe here

Elisabetta Parisi

Ground Turkey Recipes provides a valuable resource of tasty exciting recipes using ground turkey. After using ground beef for years we are all being advised to switch to the healthier choice of ground turkey. This meat has less fat and less cholesterol than ground beef. A simple switch to ground turkey can help you avoid the modern health problems of obesity and heart disease. The switch is not, however, without problems because the texture and taste of turkey is so different to beef. This doesn't mean that it is bad, it is just different. In fact turkey is a very tasty meat indeed. What does need to happen is that our tried and tested standard recipes have to be tweaked a little in order to get the most out of them. This book contains recipes that are specially formulated to get the most out of the ground turkey. So, if you are looking for change or just some different ideas, you should definitely take a look at this book.

Made in United States
North Haven, CT
16 February 2023

32701076R00065